BAKING WITH BEANS

BAKING WITH BEANS

Make Breads, Pizzas, Pies, and Cakes with Gut-Healthy Legumes

LINA WALLENTINSON

Photos: Lennart Weibull

Translated by Ellen Hedstrom and Anette Cantagallo

Skyhorse Publishing

CONTENTS

To trick a child
or why I started baking with beans

It started with a five-year-old who loved homemade bread but was suspicious of beans. That became the inspiration for this book. Olle, who is now six years old, has always been suspicious of vegetables, especially beans, peas, and lentils; sandwiches made with homemade bread on the other hand, now that's a different story.

As editor of *Buffet* magazine, I remember we once featured a bread with chickpeas in the dough. I found the recipe, tried it, and surprisingly Olle happily munched away at his sandwich with no idea of what it was hiding. I got a taste for this style of baking and started to experiment. What about making crispbread from lentils? Or a pie crust from white beans and bread rolls from green peas?

Once I had started to get an idea of the proportions between beans, liquid, and other ingredients, the results were surprisingly good. It's hard to say exactly what function is filled by beans, peas, and lentils; in some cases, they replace some of the flour, other times some of the liquid, fat, or eggs. The main thing is that the breads turn out really moist, cookies are crunchy, bars are crispy, and brownies are chocolatey and gooey.

Here's a quick tip: serve first and explain later! I promise you that your guests won't be able to guess your secret ingredients—and that includes everyone from suspicious five-year-olds to skeptical old ladies and gentlemen.

Lina

PS

However hard I try I struggle to embrace the word "legumes." Beans, peas, and lentils sound so much tastier! Sometimes when I am writing generally about legumes I might just say "beans," but remember to include peas and lentils too. It just gets tedious to keep repeating them all the time. You might come across a few "legumes" as I am trying to get used to the word, albeit reluctantly.

MORE BEANS IN YOUR BREAD

Give your health a leg up by baking with beans. Smuggle some peas into your bread rolls, spice up your crispbread, and make bars with lentils. Beans in your dough make it moist and soaked lentils give cookies, granola, and piecrust a nice crunch.

Why bake with beans?

Bread is something most of us eat every day. There's breakfast of course, a piece of crispbread as a snack, some baguette with your lunchtime soup, and maybe a sandwich before going to bed. No one should be dissing bread; lots of types of whole meal flour, whole grains, seeds, and nuts are great. It's the white breads that are low in fiber that we need to be careful of as most contain fast-acting carbohydrates, which quickly raise the blood sugar. It's fine to eat white bread now and again, but if we eat a lot of bread, we can increase its health benefits by adding beans.

Beans, peas, and lentils add protein and good fiber, but also many vitamins and minerals. There won't be a huge amount in one or two sandwiches, but still, every time you eat one you will get a boost. In addition, you reduce the peak in blood sugar that the carbohydrates in bread can cause. This is because the fibers in the legumes are the first to be broken down when they come into contact with bacteria in the large intestines.

Baking with beans is also a smart health choice in terms of protein. Protein in grains and protein in legumes look different but the body needs them all. When we eat them all together, they complement each other and are better for the body than if we eat them separately.

We need five handfuls, or around a pound of fruit and vegetables a day if you follow official guidelines. Most people eat a lot less than this. These handfuls also include beans, peas, and lentils and we are hardly consuming a lot of these either—around 12 grams a day is all we can manage when it comes to legumes.* This is another reason why baking bread with beans is so good in my opinion—also cookies, pancakes, and pizza dough!

Beans, peas, and lentils offer a lot of nutrition for little money. The best and cheapest way is to buy them dried, cook up a big batch, freeze them, and use them as and when you need them for baking. I would be lying if I told you that I was able to soak, cook, and freeze whole packages of beans just waiting to be used, but I also won't hide the fact that I feel incredibly (annoyingly) clever when I manage to cook a huge batch of beans.

If nothing else, my miserly side gets a huge pat on the back, as the price for dried beans is cheaper than a can of cooked beans. Taking into account that cooked beans is one of the cheaper things you can buy, it's obvious isn't it? If you've decided to cook your own beans, my advice is to soak the whole package at once. Do it straight away before you change your mind and start to measure and so on. Yes of course you will have lots

and lots of beans as they swell, but once you get started you may as well keep going.

Don't forget you are also being kind to the environment cooking one large batch rather than lots of small ones. It only works if you have space in the freezer of course, or plan to make lots of different meals at once such as bean soup, stews, hummus, etc.

All around the world there are several examples of how to bake using beans, peas, and lentils, mainly using flour made from legumes.

In India, crispy papadums are made from chickpea flour. Italy has its farinata, and in the south of France they call it socca; both are types of chickpea pancakes. In Asia there are lots of sweet baked goods that use beans, among other things red adzuki beans. Even in Sweden, at least in the past, legumes were used for baking. Beans and peas were used in the same way that algae and bark were—to dilute flour and make it go further. In Jämtland, Hälsingland, and Dalarna (regions in Sweden), people still make "pea" bread, a type of bread where the flour is mixed with ground yellow peas. A few local mills still grind yellow peas for flour even today.

National food 200–11, Food and nutrition consumption among Swedish adults. National Food Agency.

How to bake with beans

Soft breads

Cooked beans, peas, and lentils work best when making bread dough. More accurately you mix them with water or another liquid, which is then added to the rest of the ingredients for the dough. I often add any yeast that is needed into the smooth bean paste and then quickly mix it again so that the yeast dissolves.

Cooked beans and peas work best when mixed completely smooth. It doesn't really add any flavor, but rather adds to the moistness and of course adds health benefits. Lentils can be used in the same way, but I prefer to soak the lentils and mix them into the dough whole. You can cook them for a while if you like, just to soften them.

Recipes with soaked lentils include more liquid because they absorb more liquid during the baking process than cooked lentils. Soaked mung beans are also great to bake with. They are so small that they add some bite, just like seeds or whole grains.

If there is one thing I always keep in my freezer, it's green peas; they are perfect for baking. Just defrost them and mix into the liquid for the dough. The dough will turn a chlorophyll green, but don't be disappointed when you take it out of the oven and all the green has disappeared! The sweet taste of peas will still be there though. Green peas are also perfect to mix into pancake batter, and if you don't fry the pancakes at too high heat, the green color will remain.

Cooked white beans or chickpeas are also perfect to add to pancake dough; it doesn't add flavor but makes the pancakes healthier with a higher fiber content.

Crispbreads

If you want to bake classic crispbreads or crackers, and not include seeds, it is better to bake with cooked beans and combine with a flour such as oat flour. It's the same when making a piecrust—it will be crispier if you mix cooked beans, oat flour, and olive oil.

Soaked lentils on the other hand are perfect if you want to make a seeded crispbread. The lentils retain the shape and are soft but still have some bite.

Rinse the lentils and let them soak overnight, for at least twelve hours but preferably longer. Pour into a sieve, discarding the water, and rinse. Leave to drain before using.

If you have a sudden urge to bake crispbreads, you can do a quick soak. Rinse the dried lentils and place in a bowl. Pour boiling water on top (at least 2 cups of water per ½ cup lentils) and leave them to soak for an hour. If you have a sensitive stomach, you are better off soaking them for longer in cold water as some of the substances that can irritate the stomach are broken down.

Defrosted peas can be used to make crispbread and add some sweetness. You can even combine them with spices such as star anise and fennel. Peas contain more liquid than soaked lentils so you don't need to add as much liquid to the dough. Just like soft bread, crispbread also loses its lovely green color in the oven.

Bars, cookies, and cakes

Soaked lentils are perfect when making bars and energy balls. Just like nuts and seeds, they add crispiness as well as protein. To get the right texture, roast or fry the soaked lentils in a frying pan for ten minutes, or roast them in the oven. Soaked lentils can also be used to make crumbles, where they also add a nice crispy texture.

When making cookies and cakes you want a smooth texture, so cooked beans, lentils, or peas work best.

Gluten-free baking

In our family we mainly eat gluten-free as my oldest daughter is gluten intolerant. At the beginning it was hard to make these dietary changes when we realized how much gluten food actually contains. Despite trying to eat a varied diet, bread and pasta had become a staple that we took for granted.

It's hard having to constantly think about what we eat, but the changes have mainly been positive. We eat more interesting and varied food and discovered lots of alternatives to pasta such as buckwheat, barley, quinoa, sorghum, and millet. Learning to bake bread in a new way has been, in hindsight, both enlightening and exciting.

Usually I don't recommend a totally gluten-free diet unless you have to. Grains with gluten such as rye, corn, and wheat have gained an unwarranted bad reputation. They contain lots of healthy properties, but to get these you need to eat the whole grain. It is when you remove the husk, which is rich in fiber, and then sift away the germ, just like when you make regular flour, that the product becomes nutrient poor.

When baking you can't get away from the fact that it is easier to succeed with gluten in the bread than without.

Obviously, you can make great bread without gluten too, and just like in baked goods containing gluten, beans, lentils, and peas add moisture.

In gluten-free breads you need to replace the amazing properties that gluten contains to give the dough structure so that the air that is created during the proofing process is retained. In my recipes I tend to use fiber husk, which is ground psyllium husk. Husk has the ability to bind liquid and can be found in various grinds. In this book I mainly use the finely ground type.

Another way to get the dough light and airy is to add xanthan gum. It's a white powder that is produced through fermentation. Xanthan gum does the same job as the tough gluten threads, which is to retain the air bubbles formed in the proofing process.

Gluten-free loaves made with baking soda instead of yeast are easy to make. You could add cooked beans into the batter but I think it tastes even better to add whole soaked lentils or mung beans, which gives a nice bite to the texture.

Rolled oats and oat flour are brilliant to bake with whether you eat gluten-free or not. Thanks to the gel-like fibers (imagine porridge and you know what I mean), oat is good at binding the liquid and making a moist bread. Oat in itself does not contain gluten but it can have gluten in it from the harvesting process or if it has been handled together with wheat, rye, or barley. If you want to be totally sure that it is gluten-free, choose pure oats. In this book, recipes that are gluten-free are labeled.

Buy ready-made or make your own?

You can make bread with ready-made lentils, peas, and beans just as well as using ones you have cooked yourself. Of course it's

easier to just buy a can of beans and start baking!

The recipes in this book use ready-made beans, peas, and lentils; this is to make it as easy as possible to bake. Most ready-made legumes can be found in 14-ounce cans. This weight includes the liquid. The drained weight is around 7¾–8½ ounces. If you are cooking your own it is easy to measure out the same amounts.

How to cook legumes

All dried beans and peas work best when soaked. Place them in lots of water, at least three times the amount of beans. You can soak them overnight for at least twelve hours but up to twenty-four hours is even better. You can also reduce the cooking time by soaking them longer.

Take into account that dried legumes that are soaked and then cooked roughly double in volume, so ¼ cup of dried beans yields around ½ cup cooked.

Rinse the soaked beans in a colander and place in a large pot with lots of water. Bring to a boil and remove any foam that appears with a spoon. Add salt—around 1 teaspoon salt per 4 cups water is usually enough. Simmer on low heat under a lid so that the water is barely bubbling; this allows the beans to retain their shape. If you boil on

high heat they are more likely to break, get mushy, and lose their skin.

Cook the beans according to package instructions. Lots of things can affect cooking time such as the age of the beans, how they've been stored, and how long they have soaked for. It's best to taste a bean now and again as you're cooking. The beans should be soft but not mushy.

Leave the beans to cool in the water and they will retain their shape better. Then carefully drain the water.

Lentils don't need to soak before cooking but they offer better nutritional value if you do (see chapter on nutrients, page 20).

I prefer soaked lentils overcooked as I think they provide a better consistency and chewiness. Lentils contain low levels of antinutrients (see chapter on nutrients, page 20) so to be safe, they should not only be soaked but also heated before eating.

Red lentils cook the fastest and can easily get mushy, so I tend to err on the side of caution when following the cooking times on the package instructions and go for slightly less. Compared to beans I also discard the water straightaway and rinse the red lentils in cold water to stop the cooking process.

Green lentils come in both big and small sizes. The big green lentils also have a tendency to overcook, although not as easily as the red ones. I prefer just to soak them (read more about green lentils in the next section).

Small green lentils like Puy lentils on the other hand keep their shape when cooked. They have a firm consistency, aren't floury, and have a slightly nutty taste.

Small black lentils also keep their shape when cooked.

What bean, pea, or lentil works with what?

....

Beans

Pinto beans

The brown bean is the most Swedish of beans! It is still grown there, especially on the island of Öland. They give a nice color to bread and can be used instead of butter beans and chickpeas as well as kidney beans and black beans in brownies, cookies, and banana bread.

Kidney beans

A wine-colored red bean that got its name because it looks a bit like a kidney. Adzuki is a similar red bean but smaller (it's related to the mung bean). Both give off less color than you might think but work better in darker breads than lighter ones. Good in sweet, darker baked goods such as brownies, chocolate cookies, and banana bread.

Mung beans

Small green beans that work best when soaked and kept whole. Just like all beans they need to be heated in some way, for example through baking bread, crispbread, or bars. If you have some left over, leave the beans to sprout by keeping them in a colander for 2 to 3 days and rinsing twice a day.

Black beans

An obvious choice for anything chocolatey, but also works in dark breads and other dark baked goods. Perfect in brownies and cookies. Black beans can stain so don't cook them together with other beans.

Soybeans

The most protein-rich of all beans. It looks very much like a pea when dried but swells into an oval bean when soaked. Use in the same way as other white beans and chickpeas. When fresh, soybeans are green and they can be bought frozen too. Frozen soybeans can be used in the same way as green peas.

White beans

Large and small butter beans are used in the same way as there is no difference in taste or properties when baking. The same goes for cannellini beans, the small white beans often used in Tuscan cooking. Black-eyed peas are white but have a small black dot, hence the name.

Peas

Yellow split peas

Another Swedish classic with a nice sweet taste. Works perfectly to bake bread with or mix into a pancake dough. Cook the peas until they are soft but not mushy and you can substitute the same amount in recipes using chickpeas instead.

Green peas

Frozen green peas can be used in so many ways. Just defrost and mix into a pancake batter, a bread dough, or when making crispbread. The peas add sweetness but sadly most of the color disappears when heated.

Chickpeas

A nutty taste and firmer consistency than most cooked beans. It works in most types of breads, cookies, and cakes. Bought, ready-made chickpeas also have a unique property, as the liquid from the can (called aquafaba) can be whisked to a firm foam and used to make meringue. A special combination of protein and starch in the aquafaba helps it act in the same way as egg whites.

Lentils

Green lentils

Green lentils can be found in various varieties. The larger ones are flatter and have a tendency to break when cooked and also have a floury consistency. When cooked they add a great taste to bread. If you want more of a crunchy texture, it's better to soak them and mix into the dough before baking the bread in the oven. Small green lentils, such as Puy lentils, can be soaked and either baked with straightaway or cooked first. When cooked they retain their nice, firm consistency.

Red lentils

These are my favorite lentils! Mainly due to the color, of course. When baking I prefer only to soak them as they can easily break when cooked. They work well in bars, crumbles, crispbread, and bread. Most red lentils sold in stores are already divided into two, meaning they break even faster when cooked. A few brands sell whole lentils, so look at them in the packaging before you buy.

Black lentils

Small black lentils, or beluga lentils, keep their shape when cooked, have a nice texture, and are not floury. When cooked they look like small, shiny pearls or Russian caviar, hence the name. Soaked and roasted they add a nice crispy texture to bars and granola.

Beans—a nutritional jackpot

From a nutrient perspective, peas, beans, and lentils really are too good to be true. Legumes don't only give nutrients to those of us who eat them, but also leave some in the earth in which they grow so that the next bean sprout to grow the following year benefits. They include lots of properties the body needs such as proteins, fibers, healthy carbohydrates, vitamins, and minerals.

In short, it is hard to imagine a plant that gives more. However, just like everything else in life that seems perfect at first sight, legumes also have a darker side, especially dried beans and peas. They contain substances that can cause stomach upset and that can hinder the absorption of certain nutrients. Luckily you can avoid this by soaking and cooking the dried peas or beans until they are soft.

Another alternative is to buy ready-cooked legumes at the store. Then you just have to open the packaging, pour the contents into a sieve, and rinse with cold water. You can mix it into bread dough, cookie dough, or wherever you want to use it.

Protein

Protein is required in all body cells and is vital for the production of important hormones and enzymes.

Peas, beans, and lentils are known to contain more protein than most other plants. This is important to know, especially for vegetarians.

Proteins are large molecules that contain several parts. How the protein molecules are combined is important to the way in which the body can use it. Animal protein is the easiest to absorb and can be found in milk, meat, and other animal products. Proteins in legumes and grains have different constitutions, but when you eat them in the same meal, they complement each other, which means they have a greater value for the body than if you ate them separately.

With beans and grains in the bread you get a good combination of different proteins. Many dishes from all over the world contain a mixture of legumes and grains, for example falafel in pita bread and Indian lentil curry with naan bread.

Cooked soybeans, yellow split peas, and red and green lentils contain around 10 grams of protein per 100 grams. This means they top the list of the most protein-rich legumes. The others have between 6 to 9 grams. Cooked green peas have the lowest protein levels with 6 grams per 100 grams.

Our need for protein varies depending on how much energy, or calories, we expend. An adult who is mainly in a stationary work role needs 50 to 70 grams of protein per day. This amount can easily be gotten through eating a typical day's worth of food so it is quite unusual for most people to suffer from a lack of protein.

Carbohydrates

Beans, peas, and lentils contain a type of carbohydrate that increases blood sugar slower than those found in white bread, sugar, and pasta. Legumes have a low

glycemic index (GI). This is because they don't contain any sugar but rather other carbohydrates and fibers that the body can't metabolize as fast. There are mostly soluble fibers in legumes, and these contribute to a more even blood sugar level that reduces cholesterol levels. The fibers aren't really broken down in the gut but are used to feed the bacteria that live in the large intestine, also known as prebiotics. Bacteria convert the fibers to short-chained fatty acids that provide nutrients for the gut membrane. There are many scientific studies that show how these fibers can protect against cancer in the large intestine and rectum.

There is even resistant starch in legumes. This is a type of carbohydrate that acts like a fiber, which means it doesn't get broken down until it reaches the large intestine where it acts like food for the bacteria living there.

Cooked white beans and chickpeas contain the most fiber with around 12 grams per 100 grams. Black, red, and pinto beans contain around 6 grams per 100 grams. A healthy amount for adults is around 25 to 35 grams of fiber per day. This is more than most of us eat.

Fat

Cooked beans, lentils, and peas are low in fat. Most contain around 1 percent fat. There are a few exceptions like cooked soybeans, which contain nearly 6 percent, and chickpeas, which contain 3 percent. The peanut is also a legume and the fat content in roasted peanuts is high at 49 percent.

Vitamins

There are mainly water-soluble vitamins in legumes such as thiamine, riboflavin, niacin, and vitamin B_6. Riboflavin can be found mainly in milk, meat, and other animal products, so for vegetarians it's important to get riboflavin from other sources such as beans, peas, and lentils.

Minerals

Legumes contain several vital minerals. Calcium is needed to build bones and teeth as well as for the coagulation of blood and nerve functioning. Soybeans, white beans, and chickpeas are especially rich in calcium with 73 milligrams calcium per 100 grams cooked soybeans and around 50 milligrams in the same amount of white beans and chickpeas. The daily intake for an adult should be 800 milligrams calcium.

Soybeans are also at the top of the list when it comes to magnesium with 88 milligrams per 100 milligrams cooked soybeans. For red and white beans as well as green lentils, the levels are about 50 milligrams per 100 grams. Iron is another vital mineral we need, and there are 3.2 milligrams of iron in 100 grams cooked, green lentils. Red lentils, white beans, and soybeans contain 2.7 milligrams. Red lentils come in at a lower 1.8 milligrams per 100 grams but they are at the top the list when it comes to zinc.

The minerals in legumes are not as easy for the body to process when compared to animal products. This is because they contain phytic acid which binds to the minerals and makes them hard for the digestive system to process. By soaking legumes you can reduce the levels of phytic acid, and even more of this acid disappears when cooked.

What happens during cooking?

By soaking dried beans and peas you reduce the levels of antinutrients such as phytic acid and other substances that prevent the body from absorbing important vitamins and minerals. Lentils do not need to be soaked as they have much lower levels of these substances. You can of course make dried beans soft by just boiling them without soaking first, but then you lose out on the breaking down of the antinutrients. Leave dried peas and beans to soak for at least twelve hours before cooking them, preferably longer.

Another benefit with soaking is that oligosaccharides, which are the common carbohydrates that can be found in legumes that can cause bloating, are also affected. Always discard the water after soaking. The carbohydrates are also positively affected by cooking, which can result in a calmer stomach.

Cooking the beans, peas, or lentils will make them soft, and offers nutritional value as well. Cooking releases unwanted substances, which is why you need lots of water in the pot, making sure it completely covers the legumes.

Lectin is part of a group of undesirable substances called antinutrients. Lectin is a protein that can cause nausea but is destroyed by the cooking process. Phytic acids and tannins are other examples of negative substances that are drastically reduced by cooking. Discard the water after cooking as some of the antinutrients can still remain.

Lentils contain less antinutrients compared with beans and peas but they should still undergo some type of heat process such as baking.

Salting the water before cooking makes the beans softer, which can be important if you live in an area where the water is hard and rich in calcium. If you add something acidic to the water it can take the beans longer to soften, but it can be quicker if you add a base such as baking soda. The drawback with using baking soda is that it can give off a slightly soapy taste.

CRISPBREAD & GRANOLA

Soaked lentils are perfect when making thin and crispy breads. Or why not make a spicy crispbread from green peas? Soaked lentils are also perfect to roast together with nuts, seeds, and grains to make a crunchy granola.

Red lentil crisp bread
with chili & cumin (GLUTEN-FREE)

Why are there so many crispbreads based on seeds but none on lentils? Surely this could work, I thought, and started to experiment. After many attempts I worked it out—soaked lentils rather than cooked ones. It gives a nice light and crispy finish, almost like crackers.

1 pan

⅓ cup dried lentils (60 grams)

¼ cup flax seeds

⅔ cup pumpkin seeds

1½ tablespoons psyllium husk

¾ teaspoon salt

½ teaspoon chili flakes

1½ teaspoons cumin

1 tablespoon olive oil

¾ cup boiling water

Flaked salt to sprinkle on top (optional)

Instructions:

1. Rinse the lentils and soak overnight, or for at least 12 hours.
2. Heat the oven to 350°F.
3. Discard the water and rinse the lentils, leaving them to drain thoroughly.
4. Mix all the dry ingredients and the lentils in a bowl.
5. Add oil and water and mix thoroughly.
6. Roll out the dough thinly, placing it between two pieces of parchment paper. Lift it onto a baking pan and remove the top layer of parchment paper. Sprinkle some flaked salt on top if you like.
7. Bake in the lower part of the oven for 30 minutes. Remove the pan, turn the bread, remove the bottom layer of parchment paper, and bake for a further 5 to 10 minutes or until the bread is crunchy.
8. Leave it to cool on a cooling rack before breaking into bits.

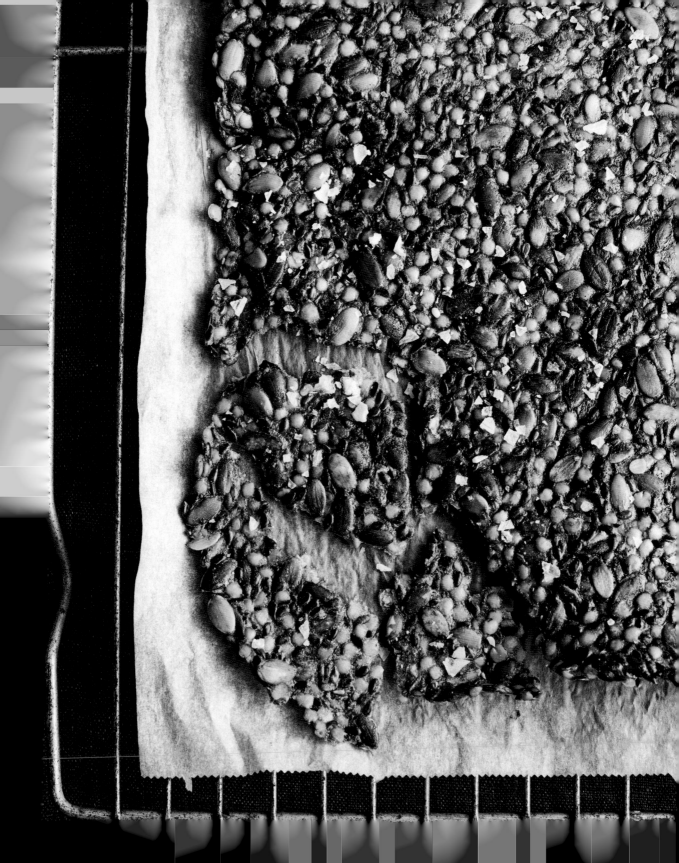

Black lentil crispbread (GLUTEN-FREE)

Black lentils, and preferably black sesame seeds, make a dramatic and crunchy crisp bread. In our house we call it ghost bread.

1 pan
½ cup dried black lentils
¼ cup chia seeds
½ cup sunflower seeds
¼ cup sesame seeds, preferably black
1½ tablespoons psyllium husk
1 teaspoon salt
1 teaspoon dried rosemary
2 tablespoons olive oil
¾ cup boiling water

Instructions:

1. Rinse the lentils and soak overnight or for at least 12 hours.
2. Heat the oven to 350°F.
3. Discard the water and rinse the lentils, leaving them to drain thoroughly.
4. Mix all the dry ingredients together with the lentils in a bowl.
5. Add oil and water and mix thoroughly.
6. Roll the dough out thinly between two pieces of parchment paper. Place on a baking pan and remove the top layer of parchment paper.
7. Bake in the lower part of the oven for around 30 minutes. Remove the pan, turn the bread, and remove the bottom layer of parchment paper. Bake for another 5 to 10 minutes or until the bread is dry and crunchy.
8. Leave to cool on a cooling rack before breaking it into bits.

Green pea crispbread
with fennel (GLUTEN-FREE)

The green peas add flavor, good fibers, and a nice color. And of course some sweetness, which works well with the spicy fennel seeds.

1 pan

5.3 ounces frozen green peas (150 grams)
½ cup boiling water
1 teaspoon fennel seeds
½ cup flax seeds
¾ cup sunflower seeds
¼ cup sesame seeds
2 teaspoons psyllium husk
1 teaspoon herb salt
1 tablespoon olive oil
½ teaspoon flaked salt to sprinkle on top

Instructions:

1. Heat the oven to 350°F.
2. Defrost the green peas. Mix peas and water by hand or with a hand blender until smooth.
3. Use a mortar and pestle to grind the fennel seeds.
4. Mix the fennel and the rest of the dry ingredients in a bowl.
5. Add the pea mixture and oil into the seed mix and mix thoroughly.
6. Roll out the dough between two pieces of parchment paper. Lift onto a baking pan and remove the top layer of parchment paper.
7. Bake in the lower part of the oven for around 20 minutes.
8. Remove the pan, turn the bread, and remove the bottom layer of parchment paper. Bake for another 10 minutes. Remove and leave to cool on a cooling rack before breaking into bits. Serve with some cream cheese.

Sesame sticks
with oats and chickpeas (GLUTEN-FREE)

Cut the dough into thin strips. The crispbread works well as a snack or served with a large piece of cheese. If you want bigger pieces of bread, you can cut them into larger pieces.

1 pan

1 (14.5 ounce) can cooked chickpeas
    (380 grams, drained weight around
    230 grams)
⅔ cup rolled oats (55 grams)
¼ cup flax seeds
1 tablespoon psyllium husk
2 pinches salt
¼ cup olive oil
½ cup boiling water
¼ cup sesame seeds
2 pinches flaked salt

Instructions:
1. Heat the oven to 350°F.
2. Remove the brine from the chickpeas, then rinse and drain them.
3. Place the chickpeas, rolled oats, flax seeds, psyllium husk, and salt in a food processor and blend until the mixture resembles breadcrumbs.
4. Add in oil and boiling water and blend again to make a smooth dough.
5. Place the dough between two pieces of parchment paper. Roll the dough out all the way to the edges of the paper. Remove the top layer of paper and sprinkle some sesame seeds and flaked salt on top of the dough. Place the paper back on top and with your hands lightly press the seeds and salt into the dough. Remove the top paper again.
6. Using a dough scraper or a knife cut into long sticks.
7. Pull the parchment paper with the dough onto a baking pan and bake in the center of the oven for 35 to 40 minutes.
8. Remove the pan and break the bread apart.
9. Leave to cool on a cooling rack.

Arugula pesto—see page 78.

Parmesan crackers (GLUTEN-FREE)

Crunchy crackers made with white beans, sorghum flour, and Parmesan cheese.

30–40 crackers

1 (14.5 ounce) can cooked white beans (380 grams, drained weight around 230 grams)

½ cup sorghum flour (50 grams)

½ tablespoon psyllium husk

½ teaspoon baking powder

1 pinch salt

¼ cup olive oil

2–3 tablespoons boiling water

1¼ cups grated Parmesan cheese

½ cup black sesame seeds

Instructions:

1. Discard the brine, then rinse and drain the beans.
2. Place the beans, sorghum flour, psyllium husk, baking powder, and salt in a food processor and blend until the mixture resembles breadcrumbs.
3. Add in oil and boiling water and mix again to make a smooth dough. Add in the cheese and give it another quick mix.
4. Make the dough into a roll shape, around 1½ inches in diameter. Sprinkle the black sesame seeds onto a piece of parchment paper and roll the dough in the seeds, pressing lightly to make the seeds stick evenly.
5. Place the roll in the freezer for around one hour.
6. Heat the oven to 350°F.
7. Remove the roll and cut it into ⅛-inch thin slices.
8. Place the slices on two baking pans covered in parchment paper. Bake one pan at a time in the middle of the oven for around 20 to 30 minutes.

Beetroot chips
with Dijon (GLUTEN-FREE)

It's hard to guess the ingredients in this pink chip: white beans, beetroot, and rolled oats. A spoonful of Dijon mustard makes it an even stranger combination but the result is crunchy and delicious.

2 pans

¾ lb. (2 whole) beetroots (350 grams)

1 (14.5 ounce) can cooked white beans
(380 grams, drained weight around
230 grams)

¾ cup rolled oats (70 grams)

2 teaspoons psyllium husk

1½ teaspoons Dijon mustard

2 tablespoons olive oil

1½ teaspoons salt

½ cup shelled hemp seeds (or sesame seeds)

Instructions:

1. Heat the oven to 300°F.
2. Boil the beetroots until soft. Discard the water, rinse in cold water, leave to cool, and then remove the skin.
3. Remove the brine from the beans, then rinse and leave to drain.
4. Divide the beetroots into smaller pieces.
5. Place the beans, beetroots, rolled oats, psyllium husk, mustard, oil, and salt in a food processor. Blend until smooth.
6. Divide the mixture across two pieces of parchment paper and smooth out evenly with a spatula. Divide the parchment paper and dough across two baking pans and sprinkle some hemp seeds on top.
7. Bake one at a time in the lower part of the oven for around 30 minutes. Remove, turn the bread, and gently remove the parchment paper. Bake for another 15 minutes. Once cooled, break into pieces.

Chocolate granola
with black lentils (GLUTEN-FREE)

The soaked lentils get crispy when roasted in the oven. It might sound odd with chocolate in the granola but try it! Cacao nibs add a heavenly taste without being too sweet.

3 cups

½ cup dried cooked black lentils (80 grams)

¾ cup rolled oats (70 grams)

½ cup pumpkin seeds

½ cup chopped nuts, e.g. pistachio, pecan, or walnuts

¼ cup flax seeds

¼ cup cacao nibs

1 teaspoon flaked salt

¼ cup canola oil

¼ cup honey

¼ cup chopped dried fruit, e.g. mango, apricot, cranberry, and fig (optional)

Instructions:

1. Rinse the lentils and leave to soak overnight or for 12 hours.
2. Heat the oven to 350°F.
3. Leave the lentils to drain thoroughly. Then, mix them in a bowl with the rolled oats, pumpkin seeds, nuts, flax seeds, cacao nibs, and flaked salt.
4. Add canola oil and honey and blend well.
5. Pour mixture out onto a baking pan covered in parchment paper and roast at the bottom of the oven for 30 to 40 minutes. Stir the mixture occasionally so it doesn't burn. If the granola starts to catch too much color toward the end of the baking time, you can cover it with a second pan.
6. Leave to cool. Meanwhile, cut the dried fruit into smaller pieces and stir into the cooled granola. Store in an airtight container.

Spicy lentil granola
with buckwheat (GLUTEN-FREE)

A super crunchy granola with both red lentils and whole buckwheat as well as lots of warming spices.

2 pints

½ cup dried red lentils

½ cup whole buckwheat

½ cup desiccated coconut

¾ cup sunflower seeds

¾ mixed nuts, e.g. hazelnuts, cashews, or walnuts

¼ cup chia seeds

1 teaspoon flaked salt

2 teaspoons ground cinnamon

1 teaspoon ground cardamom

½ teaspoon ground ginger

¼ cup canola oil

¼ cup honey

¾ cup dried fruit, e.g. apricot, pomegranate seeds, figs, cranberries, raisins

Instructions:

1. Rinse the lentils and place them to soak overnight or for at least 12 hours. Rinse the buckwheat in really hot water for around 30 seconds, then rinse in cold water and soak overnight or for at least 8 hours (or soak in boiling water for one hour).
2. Heat the oven to 350°F.
3. Rinse the lentils and buckwheat and drain thoroughly.
4. In a separate bowl mix the lentils and buckwheat with desiccated coconut, sunflower seeds, nuts, chia seeds, flaked salt, and spices.
5. Add canola oil and honey and mix thoroughly.
6. Pour out onto a baking pan covered in parchment paper and roast at the bottom of the oven for 30 to 40 minutes. Stir the mixture occasionally so it doesn't burn. If the granola starts to catch too much color toward the end of the baking time, you can cover it with a second pan.
7. Leave to cool. Meanwhile, chop the dried fruit into smaller pieces and stir into the cooled granola.
8. Store in an airtight container.

BREAD

Give rolls a boost with green peas, bake crazy pink breads with beetroot and white beans in the dough, or make simple loaves with buttermilk, adding soaked mung beans and lentils to make them nice and chewy.

Buckwheat squares (GLUTEN-FREE)

Buckwheat is a bit different with its nutty and almost grassy taste. Either you like it or you don't—but I do! Despite its name the flour is completely gluten-free. If you choose pure rolled oats this makes a great gluten-free bread.

20 squares

1 (14.5 ounce) can cooked kidney beans
     (380 grams, drained weight around
     230 grams)
2 cups cold water
25 grams fresh yeast (or 6 grams dry yeast)
1½ cups buckwheat flour (175 grams)
1½ tablespoons psyllium husk
2 teaspoons xanthan gum
1½ teaspoons salt
1¼ cups rolled oats (105 grams)
2 tablespoons honey
2 tablespoons olive oil
¼ cup hemp seeds to sprinkle on top
     (optional)

Instructions:

1. Remove the brine, then rinse the beans and leave to drain. By hand or using a hand blender mix the beans and water into a smooth paste. Add the yeast and mix briefly to dissolve.
2. In a separate bowl mix the buckwheat flour, psyllium husk, xanthan gum, salt, and rolled oats.
3. To the bean paste add the flour mix, honey, and oil. Mix into a smooth dough; it should be slightly sticky.
4. Using a spatula, spread the dough out in a greased 12 x 8-inch ovenproof dish.
5. Sprinkle hemp seeds on top (optional) and cut into 20 squares. Cover the dough and leave to proof for around 3 hours.
6. Heat the oven to 450°F.
7. Bake in the middle of the oven for around 30 minutes. Leave for 15 minutes in the dish before taking the bread out and cooling on a cooling rack.

Green pea bread rolls with fennel

I often keep green peas in the freezer as they are great for making bread rolls. These rolls are a special favorite of my six-year-old son, Olle, the family's biggest pea skeptic, when I call them Hulk rolls.

20 rolls

½ lb. frozen green peas (250 grams)

¾ cup cold water

12 grams fresh yeast (or 3 grams dry yeast)

2 teaspoons fennel

1 tablespoon olive oil

1 teaspoon salt

2½ cups flour (360 grams)

Sesame seeds and fennel seeds for sprinkling

Instructions:

1. Defrost the peas. Mix them into a smooth paste together with the water by hand or using a hand blender. Add the yeast and mix quickly until it dissolves.
2. Grind the fennel seeds in a mortar and pestle.
3. Mix all the ingredients in a bowl to make a loose dough.
4. Cover the dough and proof at room temperature for around 2 hours or until the dough doubles in size.
5. Tip the dough onto a floured surface but don't knead it. Slowly pull out the dough and split it into 20 pieces. Place the pieces on a baking pan covered in parchment paper, then cover and proof for around one hour.
6. Heat the oven to 450°F.
7. Carefully brush the rolls with a little water and sprinkle some sesame and fennel seeds on top.
8. Bake in the middle of the oven for around 15 minutes or until the rolls have turned a nice color.

Pink beetroot bread

There's a slightly hippie feel to this bread. I mean, who expects pink bread? The beetroot juice and white beans combine to create this crazy color.

2 small loaves

1 (14.5 ounce) can cooked white beans
      (380 grams, drained weight around
      230 grams)
½ cup cold water
⅔ cup beetroot juice
12 grams yeast (or 3 grams dry yeast)
2¾ cups sifted spelt flour, or all-purpose flour
      (420 grams)
1 tablespoon olive oil
1½ teaspoons salt
Flaked salt for sprinkling

Instructions:

1. Discard the brine, then rinse and thoroughly drain the beans. By hand or with a hand blender combine the beans, water, and beetroot juice into a smooth paste. Add the yeast and quickly blend again until it dissolves.

2. Pour the bean paste into a bowl and add the rest of the ingredients. Mix into a loose dough. Cover the dough and leave to proof at room temperate for around 3 hours or until the dough has doubled in size.

3. Gently tip the dough onto a floured surface but don't knead it. Halve the dough and make two round breads. Place the breads on a baking pan covered with parchment paper and make a couple of scores in the loaves using a sharp knife. Sprinkle some flaked salt on top.

4. Leave to proof under cover for around one hour or until the bread has roughly doubled in size.

5. Heat the oven to 475°F.

6. Bake the bread in the middle of the oven for around 25 minutes or until it has turned a nice color.

Cold proofed rye bread rolls

Mix up the dough the night before and you'll have fresh rolls for breakfast.

20 rolls

2 (14.5 ounce) cans white beans or chickpeas (380 grams, drained weight around 230 grams)

1⅔ cups cold water

12 grams fresh yeast (or 3 grams dry yeast)

¾ cup dark rye flour (110 grams)

2¾ cups extra strong wheat flour (420 grams)

1 tablespoon honey

2 tablespoons olive oil

2 teaspoons salt

Flour for dusting

Instructions:

1. Discard the brine, rinse, and leave the beans to drain thoroughly. Blend the beans and water to a smooth paste by hand or with a hand blender. Add the yeast and quickly blend again until dissolved.

2. Add the rest of the ingredients. Mix to make a smooth but slightly sticky dough. Cover and leave to proof in the fridge overnight or for around 12 hours.

3. Heat the oven to 450°F.

4. Remove the dough and tip onto a floured surface. Don't knead it. Sprinkle some flour on top and cut it into 20 pieces. Place the pieces on two baking pans covered in parchment paper.

5. Leave to proof at room temperature for around one hour or until they have reached a good size.

6. Bake one at a time in the middle of the oven for 17 to 20 minutes. Leave to cool on a cooling rack.

GREEN PEA SPREAD

Mix ½ lb. defrosted green peas, ¼ cup olive oil, ½ tablespoon tahini, 1 tablespoon freshly squeezed lemon juice, 1 tablespoon freshly chopped mint, 2 pinches salt, and 1 pinch chili flakes. Sprinkle roasted sesame seeds and chopped nuts, such as pistachios, on top.

Walnut bread with green lentils

This bread is a lighter version of sourdough. The graham flour, yeast, and water are mixed into a pre-dough that is left for twenty-four hours to give the bread a lovely tangy taste.

2 small loaves
Pre-dough:
12 grams fresh yeast (or 3 grams dry yeast)
1⅔ cups graham or whole wheat flour
    (240 grams)
2 cups cold water

1 (14.5 ounce) can cooked green lentils
    (380 grams, drained weight around
    230 grams)
2¾ cups strong, white flour (420 grams)
2 tablespoons honey
1 tablespoon salt
¾ cup walnuts

Instructions:
1. Mix the yeast and flour in the water. Cover with a baking towel and leave at room temperature for 24 hours.
2. Discard the brine, rinse, and leave the lentils to drain.
3. Add the strong flour, honey, salt, and walnuts to the dough and combine. Add the lentils, cover, and proof for around 1 hour.
4. Tip the dough onto a floured surface and halve. Shape each half into a round loaf and place them on a baking pan covered in parchment paper.
5. Leave to proof for around 1 hour or until the bread has risen to a nice size.
6. Heat the oven to 475°F.
7. Bake for 15 minutes in the middle of the oven and then reduce the temperature to 450°F and bake for a further 20 to 25 minutes.
8. Leave the bread to cool on a cooling rack without a cover.

Carrot bread
with red lentils

Some people get their kicks from parachuting or driving fast cars. I get mine from seeing how many red lentils and grated carrots you can fit into a bread. To each their own!

1 loaf

Pre-dough:

12 grams fresh yeast (or 3 grams dry yeast)

1⅔ cups graham or whole wheat flour
    (240 grams)

2 cups cold water

¾ cup dried red lentils (160 grams)

2¾ cups strong, white flour (420 grams)

1¼ cups finely grated carrots (around
    120 grams)

2 tablespoons honey

2 teaspoons salt

Instructions:

1. Mix the yeast and the flour into the water. Cover with a baking towel and leave at room temperature overnight or for around 12 hours.

2. Cook the lentils according to the packaging; they should be soft but not mushy. Discard the water and drain thoroughly.

3. Add the strong flour, carrots, honey, and salt to the dough and combine. Add the lentils and combine again.

4. Tip the dough into a loaf pan covered with parchment paper, or an ovenproof dish measuring around 12 x 15 inches.

5. Leave to proof without cover for around 2 hours or until the bread has risen nicely.

6. Heat the oven to 450°F.

7. Carefully score the dough into 30 pieces.

8. Bake in the middle of the oven for 25 minutes.

9. Leave to cool on a cooling rack.

The bread picture here is half a batch in a pan measuring around 12 x 8 inches.

Casserole bread with apple & caraway

The yellow split pea will forever be associated with the slightly mushy soup, while the chickpea gets to feature in both falafel and hummus. This apple bread with a crisp and crunchy crust is my attempt to settle the score for these peas.

I large loaf

¾ cup dried yellow split peas (150 grams)
1½ cups cold water
12 grams fresh yeast (or 3 grams dry yeast)
2 teaspoons caraway seeds
3¼ cups sifted spelt flour (480 grams)
1¼ cups finely grated apple (175 grams)
2 tablespoons olive oil
2 teaspoons salt

DID YOU FORGET TO SOAK?

Truth be told you can swap the split yellow peas for white beans or chickpeas if you don't want to soak and cook them yourself. Replace the amount in this recipe for 2 cans at (14.5 ounce) 380 grams each.

WHY A CAST-IRON DISH?

It gives the same effect as a professional oven. When the casserole is heated up in advance it helps to retain an even high heat in the oven and gives the bread a professional tasting crispy crust.

Instructions:

1. Rinse and soak the peas overnight or for at least 12 hours.
2. Discard the water, rinse the peas, and cook for 30 minutes or according to package instructions. They should be soft but not mushy. Discard the water and leave the peas to drain and cool down.
3. Mix the peas and water into a smooth paste by hand or with a hand blender. Add the yeast and quickly mix until it dissolves.
4. Pour the pea paste into a bowl and mix with the rest of the ingredients into a loose dough. Cover and leave to proof for around 4 hours at room temperature.
5. Press the dough into the bowl with a lightly floured hand and leave to proof under cover for another hour.
6. Heat the oven to 450°F. Place a cast-iron Dutch oven or casserole dish in the lower part of the oven for at least 20 minutes until it gets really hot.
7. Remove the casserole dish, sprinkle some flour on the bottom, and tip the dough into the dish straightaway. Place the lid on top.
8. Bake the bread in the middle of the oven for 30 minutes. Remove the lid and bake for another 20 minutes (or until the inner temperature reaches 205°F).
9. Wait a few minutes before tipping out the bread; you can use a dinner knife to loosen it from the edges. Leave to cool on a cooling rack. The bread tastes best if you leave it to stand until the following day. Store it wrapped in a tea towel until the next day.

Plaited spelt baguettes with pistachio pesto

This bread looks a lot more advanced than it is. It is basically like a cinnamon bun except that the dough is divided lengthwise rather than cut into bun shapes. Then, all you need to do is twist.

2 baguettes
Dough

1 (14.5 ounce) can cooked white beans (380 grams, drained weight around 230 grams)
¾ cup cold water
12 grams fresh yeast (or 3 grams dry yeast)
2 cups sifted spelt flour (300 grams)
1 tablespoon olive oil
½ tablespoon honey
1 teaspoon salt
1 egg, whisked for brushing

Pesto

1 bunch basil
1 garlic clove, peeled and finely chopped
¾ cup finely grated Parmesan
½ cup pistachio nuts
¼ cup olive oil
1 pinch salt
1 pinch freshly ground black pepper

Instructions:

1. **Dough:** Discard the brine, then rinse and leave the beans to drain. Mix the beans with water into a smooth paste by hand or using a hand blender. Add the yeast and mix quickly until dissolved.
2. Pour the bean paste into a bowl and mix in the rest of the ingredients for the dough. Mix into a loose dough. Cover and leave to proof for around 4 hours at room temperature or until the dough has roughly doubled in size.

   Pesto: Mix basil leaves, garlic, Parmesan, pistachio nuts, oil, salt, and pepper by hand or with a hand blender to make a rough pesto.

1. **Roll out the bread:** Tip the dough onto a floured surface. Divide into two even pieces and roll each piece into a rectangle, around 8 x 10 inches.
2. Smooth the pesto evenly over the two pieces of dough and roll, starting from the short end, into two rolls. Cut each roll in half lengthwise (to make two lengths of each roll). Place the cut lengths with the opening facing up and twist/plait into two breads.
3. Place on a baking pan covered in parchment paper and leave to proof, uncovered, for around 1 hour.
4. Heat the oven to 400°F.
5. Carefully brush the baguettes with the whisked egg. Bake in the middle of the oven for 25 to 30 minutes. If the baguettes brown too quickly you can add a baking pan on the rack above the baguettes toward the end of the baking time.
6. Leave to cool on a cooling rack.

Focaccia with
rosemary & olives (GLUTEN-FREE)

Of course, I had to see if my usual gluten-free focaccia would work with a chickpea twist. It did! Leave the bread to rest for a while before cutting it. A lot of gluten-free breads are best when they have cooled off a bit and calmed down.

2 loaves

1 (14.5 ounce) can cooked chickpeas (380 grams, drained weight around 230 grams)

2¼ cups tepid water

25 grams fresh yeast (or 6 grams dry yeast)

4 tablespoons olive oil

1 tablespoon honey

¾ cup sorghum flour (100 grams)

1⅔ cups rice flour (200 grams)

1¼ cups potato flour (225 grams)

2 teaspoons xanthan gum

2 teaspoons salt

⅔ cup black olives

Rosemary sprigs

Instructions:

1. Remove the brine, then rinse and leave the chickpeas to drain. Mix the chickpeas into a smooth paste with the water. Add the yeast and quickly mix so that all the yeast dissolves. Add olive oil and honey to the mixture.

2. Mix sorghum flour, rice flour, potato flour, xanthan gum, and salt together. Add the pea paste and whisk with an electric whisk for around 2 minutes. The dough should be loose and sticky.

3. Divide the dough across two pieces of parchment paper and shape into two ovals with a spatula (or spread the whole dough over one baking pan covered in parchment paper).

4. Brush with olive oil and sprinkle some flaked salt on top. Press the olives into the dough and lay some rosemary sprigs on top. Leave to proof uncovered for around 2 hours.

5. Heat the oven to 475°F.

6. Bake one at a time in the middle of the oven for around 20 to 25 minutes or until the bread turns a nice color. Leave to cool on a cooling rack for around 10 minutes before cutting.

Breakfast muffins
with oats and sorghum (GLUTEN-FREE)

Using baking powder instead of yeast means these muffins are quick and easy to bake.

30 muffins

1 (14.5 ounce) can cooked white beans
   (380 grams, drained weight around
   230 grams)
2½ cups buttermilk
1⅔ cups rolled oats (140 grams)
¾ cup sorghum flour (100 grams)
4 tablespoons psyllium husk
4 teaspoons baking powder
2 teaspoons salt
3½ ounces cold butter (100 grams)
Rolled oats for sprinkling

Instructions:

1. Heat the oven to 450°F.
2. Discard the brine, then rinse and leave the beans to thoroughly drain.
3. Mix the beans into a smooth paste with the buttermilk.
4. Mix all the dry ingredients in a bowl. Add the butter in pieces and pinch together into a crumbly dough. Add the beans and quickly mix into a loose dough.
5. Leave the dough to swell for around 5 minutes. Shape into 30 balls and place into muffin liners or straight onto two baking pans covered in parchment paper. Sprinkle some rolled oats on top.
6. Bake in the middle of the oven for around 20 minutes. Leave to cool on a cooling rack.

TIP!
Shape the rolls into oblong shapes instead and sprinkle sesame seeds on top. Perfect hot dog buns!

Carrot rolls
with pumpkin seeds (GLUTEN-FREE)

The entire food pyramid in a roll? Not quite, but these rolls contain a lot of good stuff and taste delicious!

30 rolls

1 (14.5 ounce) can cooked chickpeas
(380 grams, drained weight around
230 grams)
3 cups carrot juice
1⅔ cups rolled oats (140 grams)
1½ cups sorghum flour (175 grams)
½ cup pumpkin seeds
4 tablespoons psyllium husk
4 teaspoons baking powder
1½ teaspoons salt
3½ ounces butter (100 grams)
Pumpkin seeds for sprinkling

Instructions:

1. Heat the oven to 450°F.
2. Discard the brine, then rinse and leave the chickpeas to drain. Mix the chickpeas with the carrot juice by hand or using a hand blender.
3. Mix all the dry ingredients in a bowl. Add the butter in pieces and pinch together to make a crumbly dough. Add the bean paste and quickly mix into a dough.
4. Leave the dough to swell for around 10 minutes.
5. Divide the dough in two and shape each one into a roll on a floured surface. Cut each roll into 15 pieces. Place the pieces on two baking pans covered in parchment paper. Sprinkle pumpkin seeds on top and gently press them into the dough using your hand.
6. Bake one pan at a time in the middle of the oven for around 20 minutes. Leave to cool on a cooling rack.

Simple oat bread with
mung beans and nuts (GLUTEN-FREE)

A real favorite which I've baked a lot but always with buckwheat flour. Of course I had to test swapping the buckwheat flour for mung beans—it's the kind of stuff that keeps me awake at night! It worked great.

1 loaf

½ cup dried mung beans (90 grams)

½ cup flax seeds

½ cup sesame seeds

1 tablespoon psyllium husk

¾ cup boiling water

½ cup dark syrup

1¼ cups oat flour (150 grams)

2 teaspoons baking soda

1½ teaspoons salt

⅔ cup Greek yogurt

½ cup roasted pumpkin seeds

½ cup roasted nuts, e.g. hazelnuts, almonds, walnuts

Oil for greasing

Oat flour for sprinkling

Instructions:

1. Rinse the mung beans and place them to soak overnight or for at least 12 hours.
2. Heat the oven to 400°F.
3. Mix flax seeds, sesame seeds, and psyllium husk in a large bowl.
4. Pour the boiling water over it and mix until smooth. Add the syrup and keep stirring until smooth. Leave for around 10 minutes.
5. Discard the mung bean water, rinse, and leave to drain thoroughly.
6. Mix the oat flour, baking soda, and salt in a bowl. Add the mung beans.
7. Pour the flour mix and yogurt into the seed mixture and stir until everything is blended. Add the pumpkin seeds and nuts.
8. Pour the mixture into a greased loaf pan, around 9 x 5 x 3 inches. Sprinkle some rolled oats on top.
9. Place in the lower part of the oven for around 1 hour. Cover with another baking pan if the bread is starting to brown too much toward the end.
10. Leave the bread to rest in the loaf pan for around 30 minutes before turning it out.

Lingonberry loaf
with lentils (GLUTEN-FREE)

Such a feel-good bread! Oats, buttermilk, lingonberries, chia seeds, lentils, and nuts. All the good stuff!

1 loaf

½ cup dried lentils (80 grams)

2 teaspoons whole star anise

1 teaspoon fennel seeds

1¼ cups rolled oats (150 grams)

2 teaspoons baking soda

½ cup chia seeds

½ cup sunflower seeds

1 tablespoon psyllium husk

¾ cup roasted nuts, e.g. hazelnuts, almonds, walnuts

1½ teaspoons salt

1⅔ cups buttermilk

¼ cup honey

¾ cup frozen lingonberries

Oat flour and sunflower seeds for sprinkling

Instructions:

1. Rinse the lentils and leave to soak overnight or for at least 12 hours.
2. Heat the oven to 400°F.
3. Discard the water from the lentils and leave to drain thoroughly.
4. Grind the star anise and fennel seeds in a mortar and pestle.
5. Mix the rolled oats, baking soda, chia seeds, sunflower seeds, psyllium husk, ground spices, nuts, lentils, and salt in a bowl.
6. Add in buttermilk and honey and mix into a smooth dough. Fold in the frozen lingonberries and briefly mix so the berries don't get crushed.
7. Put the mixture into a loaf pan covered in parchment paper, around 8½ x 4½ x 2½ inches.
8. Sprinkle some oat flour and sunflower seeds on top.
9. Bake in the middle of the oven for around 80 minutes. Keep an eye on it toward the end so that the crust doesn't burn. If it begins to brown too fast you can place a pan on the rack above the loaf.
10. Leave to cool for 30 minutes before removing the loaf from the pan. Leave to cool down completely on a cooling rack.

Seeded loaf with beans and caraway (GLUTEN-FREE)

A compact and solid bread that works well when sliced, frozen, and then toasted.

1 loaf

½ cup dried mung beans (90 grams)
1 tablespoon caraway seeds
¾ cup sunflower seeds
⅔ cup flax seeds
½ cup almonds
¾ cup rolled oats (70 grams)
2 tablespoons chia seeds
3 tablespoons psyllium husk
2 teaspoons salt
1¼ cups cold water
1 tablespoon honey
3 tablespoons olive oil

Instructions:

1. Rinse the mung beans and leave to soak overnight or for at least 12 hours.
2. Discard the water, rinse, and leave the beans to thoroughly drain.
3. Grind the caraway seeds in a mortar and pestle.
4. Mix all the dry ingredients in a bowl. Add mung beans and mix thoroughly.
5. Mix water with the honey and oil and pour over the seed mix.
6. Make a dough; it should be fairly dense. Press the dough into a parchment-covered loaf pan, around 8½ x 4½ x 2½ inches. Leave to rest for around 3 hours at room temperature.
7. Heat the oven to 350°F. Bake the bread in the middle of the oven for around 1 hour. Keep an eye on it so it doesn't burn. Leave to cool before turning it out of the pan.
8. Leave the bread to completely cool on a cooling rack.

BEETROOT HUMMUS
Mix 1 peeled, cooked beetroot, ½ (14.5 ounce) can of chickpeas, 1 peeled and finely chopped garlic clove, 2 tablespoons olive oil, ½ tablespoon freshly pressed lemon juice, 2 pinches salt, and 1 pinch pepper. Top off with beetroot shoots if you like.

Orange scones
with parsnips (GLUTEN-FREE)

Grated orange peel and parsnip make a great taste combination. Add some beans and you have a great breakfast with crispy, gluten-free scones.

16 pieces

1 (14.5 ounce) can cooked white beans
    (380 grams, drained weight around
    230 grams)
¾ cup oat flour (100 grams)
2 teaspoons baking powder
½ teaspoon salt
1¼ cups finely grated parsnips (around
    90 grams)
½ tablespoon finely grated orange peel
3½ ounces cold butter (100 grams)
½ cup mixed seeds, e.g. pumpkin seeds,
    sesame, and sunflower seeds

Instructions:

1. Heat the oven to 450°F.
2. Discard the brine, rinse, and leave the beans to drain.
3. Mix the beans into a smooth paste in a food processor.
4. Mix the oat flour, baking powder, and salt in a bowl. Add the grated parsnips and orange zest and mix.
5. Cut the butter into small pieces.
6. Add the flour mix and butter to a food processor and mix into a smooth dough. Push the dough down from the edges and mix again to make sure all the ingredients are mixed together.
7. Shape into four round loaves on a baking pan covered in parchment paper.
8. Sprinkle seeds on top and gently press so that the seeds stick to the bread. Score a cross over each bread.
9. Bake in the middle of the oven for around 20 minutes. Leave the bread to rest for a few minutes. They are best eaten when still a bit warm as they taste the best then.

PURE ROLLED OATS
These scones are gluten-free if you use flour made from pure oats. You can make your own oat flour by mixing pure rolled oats in a food processor.

Bread with poppy seeds

This is a lovely bread to serve with a soup or stew. If you prefer to make the dough into larger rolls, reduce the oven time by 10 minutes.

1 bread (25 to 30 rolls)

2 (14.5 ounce) cans cooked white beans or chickpeas (380 grams, drained weight around 230 grams)

1²⁄₃ cups cold water

25 grams fresh yeast (or 6 grams dry yeast)

1¼ cups rolled oats (105 grams)

3¼ cups strong, white flour (480 grams)

1 tablespoon honey

2 tablespoons olive oil

2 teaspoons salt

Flour for rolling

Butter for greasing

1 egg for brushing

2 tablespoons poppy seeds for sprinkling

Instructions:

1. Discard the brine, then rinse and leave the beans to thoroughly drain. Mix the beans into a smooth paste by hand or with a hand blender together with the water. Add the yeast and quickly mix until dissolved.

2. Pour the bean paste into a large bowl. Add rolled oats, flour, honey, oil, and salt. Mix into a smooth but slightly sticky dough. Cover and leave to proof at room temperature for around 4 hours.

3. Heat the oven to 450°F.

4. Tip the dough onto a floured surface. Divide into 25 to 30 pieces and roll each piece into a bun shape. Place the buns close together on a greased baking pan, around 12 x 12 inches in size, or straight onto a baking pan covered in parchment paper.

5. Cover and leave to proof at room temperature for around 1 hour or until they the buns have properly risen. Carefully brush with a whisked egg and sprinkle some poppy seeds on top.

6. Bake at the bottom of the oven for 25 to 30 minutes. If the bread starts to brown too much you can place another baking pan upside down on top toward the end of the baking time.

PIZZA, PIES & PANCAKES

Make a crisp piecrust with peas and rolled oats. Or a pizza base from white beans. Jazz up your pancakes with mixed green peas or fry fluffy mini pancakes made from sorghum flour and chickpeas.

Lentil & cauliflower pizza base (GLUTEN-FREE)

I like a pizza base made from grated cauliflower, eggs, and cheese. It doesn't really look like a traditional pizza base but tastes very good. The red lentils elevate it even further.

4 small pizza bases

¼ cup dried red lentils (80 grams)
1 lb. cauliflower
2 eggs
1 teaspoon dried oregano
½ teaspoon salt
1 pinch chili flakes
¾ cup grated strong cheese e.g. Parmesan or pecorino

Instructions:

1. Thoroughly rinse the lentils and leave to soak overnight or for at least 12 hours.
2. Heat the oven to 450°F.
3. Remove the cauliflower florets from the stem.
4. Finely blend the florets in a food processor. Place the cauliflower in a colander and pour 2 pints of boiling water on top. Leave to cool and squeeze as much liquid as you can out of the cauliflower.
5. Rinse the lentils and leave them to thoroughly drain. Blend the lentils in a food processor until they resemble breadcrumbs. Add the eggs, cauliflower, oregano, salt, and chili flakes. Mix together to make a dough. Add the cheese and then quickly mix again.
6. Make 4 flat rounds (around 5 inches in diameter) on a baking pan covered in parchment paper.
7. Bake in the middle of the oven for around 10 minutes or until the pizza bases are golden and crispy. Remove and add the topping to the pizza bases. Bake for another 5 minutes or until the pizzas have a nice color.

Pizza topping with goat cheese, artichokes & pesto

Bake the pizza bases with crème fraiche, artichokes, and goat cheese. Top off with soybeans and pesto.

Topping for 4 small pizzas

⅔ cup crème fraiche
¾ cup marinated artichokes
5.3 ounces goat cheese (150 grams)
A handful of soybeans or green peas, one handful of arugula, and arugula pesto (optional)

Instructions:

1. Spread the crème fraiche over the baked pizza bases. Chop the artichokes into smaller pieces and crumble the goat cheese on top.
2. Bake in the middle of the oven for 5 to 10 minutes at 450°F.
3. Sprinkle roughly mashed soybeans or green peas on top, then add arugula and a dollop of arugula pesto (see tip below) or ready-made pesto from a jar.

ARUGULA PESTO

Mix ½ cup roasted and peeled almonds, ¾ cup arugula, ¾ cup grated pecorino, 1 peeled garlic clove, grated zest of 1 lemon, ½ cup olive oil, 1 pinch of salt, and 1 pinch of pepper.

Italian pizza dough (GLUTEN-FREE)

It's a bit of a challenge to make a gluten-free pizza dough, and adding beans makes it even harder, but this one is really good! The xanthan gum helps to make the gluten-free dough fluffy.

2 small or 1 large pizza

½ (14.5 ounce) can cooked white beans
    (380 grams, drained weight around
    115 grams)
1 cup cold water
12 grams yeast (or 3 grams dry yeast)
½ cup sorghum flour (50 grams)
¾ cup rice flour (100 grams)
⅔ cup potato flour (100 grams)
1 teaspoon xanthan gum
1½ teaspoons salt
2 tablespoons olive oil
1 teaspoon honey

PIZZA TOPPINGS!

Tomato puree is a quick and easy alternative to tomato sauce. You can top it with whatever ingredients you like or happen to have at home.

    Spread ½ cup tomato puree over the pizza bases. Sprinkle 1⅔ cups grated, strong cheese on top such as Västerbotten cheese (a mature, strong-tasting cow's milk cheese from Sweden) or cheddar and add 2 red onions cut into wedges evenly across the base. If you like you can add ¼ cup black olives as well. Bake according to the recipe. Remove and sprinkle some greens such as arugula, basil, and pea shoots on top before serving.

Instructions:

1. Discard the brine, rinse, and leave the beans to drain.
2. Mix the beans and water into a smooth paste by hand or with a hand blender. Add the yeast and mix quickly until dissolved.
3. Mix the sorghum flour, rice flour, potato flour, xanthan gum, and salt together. Add in the bean paste, oil, and honey. Mix to make a loose dough.
4. Using a spatula spread the dough into two oval bases across two baking trays covered in parchment paper (or smooth the whole dough onto one baking tray covered in parchment paper to make one large rectangular-shaped pizza).
5. Leave the dough to proof without cover for 2 hours.
6. Heat the oven to 475°F.
7. Bake at the bottom of the oven for 10 minutes. Remove and add your own topping or use my suggestions below. Return to the oven and bake in the top part of the oven for another 10 minutes or until the pizza turns a nice color.

Beetroot and chickpea pie
with feta cheese & rosemary (GLUTEN-FREE)

A crispy pie shell made from chickpeas and rolled oats that is easy to mix together. You can fill it with beetroot and feta cheese or choose your own filling.

1 pie crust

1 (14.5 ounce) can cooked chickpeas (380 grams, drained weight around 230 grams)

½ cup rolled oats (35 grams)

¼ cup olive oil

½ teaspoon salt

Olive oil for greasing

Instructions:

1. Discard the brine, rinse, and leave the chickpeas to thoroughly drain.
2. Place the rolled oats in a food processor and blend into a fine flour.
3. Add chickpeas, oil, and salt. Mix into a smooth dough.
4. Press the dough into a greased pan, around 10 inches in diameter. Make sure the base is not too thin. Pat the pie edge on the inside to keep the dough from collapsing down.
5. Chill the pan for around 30 minutes.
6. Heat the oven to 400°F.
7. Bake the pie crust in the lower part of the oven for around 30 minutes. Leave to cool before adding the filling and baking.

Filling:

1 lb. small mixed beetroots, red, yellow, and polka beets

1 tablespoon olive oil

1 red onion, peeled and cut into wedges

1¾ ounces kale, chopped (50 grams)

1¼ cups Greek yogurt

3 eggs

1 tablespoon honey

¾ cup grated, strong cheese (such as cheddar)

2 teaspoons finely chopped fresh rosemary

1 teaspoon salt

½ teaspoon grated black pepper

3½ ounces feta cheese (100 grams)

Instructions:

1. Heat the oven to 400°F.
2. Place the beetroots on a baking pan and bake in the middle of the oven for around 45 minutes or until they are soft (they can bake at the same time as the pie crust). Leave to cool down a bit before peeling. Divide in half.
3. Increase the oven temperature to 450°F.
4. Place half of the beetroots, onion, and kale in the pie crust.
5. Whisk together the yogurt, eggs, honey, cheese, rosemary, salt, and pepper in a bowl. Pour the mixture into the pie crust.
6. Place the rest of the beetroot and onion into the crust. Add the rest of the kale and crumble the feta cheese on top.
7. Bake in the middle of the oven for 20 to 25 minutes or until the pie has turned a nice color.

BAKING WITH BEANS

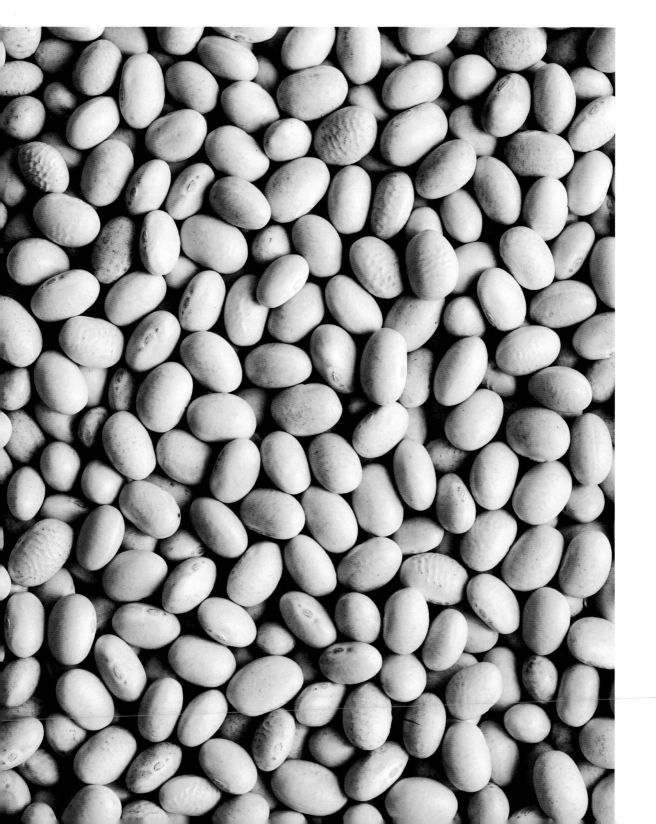

Graham pancakes with peas

Suspicious children will tell you that these green pancakes taste like … well, pancakes! The graham flour gives more of a flavor and the peas and spinach add color as well as all the health benefits.

10 pancakes

3½ ounces frozen green peas (100 grams)
½ bag fresh baby spinach (35 grams)
    (optional)
¾ cup whole milk
2 eggs
⅔ cup graham flour
½ teaspoon salt
2 tablespoons butter
More butter for frying if needed

Instructions:

1. Defrost the peas.
2. Mix the peas and spinach with half the milk by hand or using a hand blender.
3. Add the rest of the milk, eggs, graham flour, and salt. Quickly mix into a smooth batter. Leave to rest for around 5 minutes.
4. Melt the butter in a small frying pan, around 8 inches in diameter. Mix the melted butter into the batter.
5. Fry the pancakes in the frying pan, adding more butter to the pan as needed.

PANCAKE TOPPINGS!
Pancakes are great to eat with just jelly. Or you can add a dollop of crème fraiche with horseradish, peas, pea shoots, and black pepper as pictured here.

American pancakes (GLUTEN-FREE)

Puffy pancakes made from chickpeas and sorghum flour. Eat them with berries, thick yogurt, nuts, and honey.

30 small pancakes

1 (14.5 ounce) can cooked chickpeas (around
    380 grams, drained weight around
    230 grams)
1¼ cups milk
3 eggs
⅔ cup sorghum flour (75 grams)
1 teaspoon psyllium husk
1 teaspoon baking powder
½ teaspoon vanilla extract
1 tablespoon raw sugar
1 teaspoon salt
2 tablespoons butter for frying
Extra butter if needed

Instructions:

1. Discard the brine, rinse, and leave the chickpeas to drain.
2. Mix all the ingredients by hand or with a hand blender until smooth. Leave the batter to rest for 5 minutes.
3. Melt the butter in a frying pan.
4. Fry the pancakes using a frying pan that can make several mini pancakes at once. You need around 1 tablespoon of batter per pancake. Add more butter to the pan as needed. The pancakes are ready to flip when they have risen slightly and the surface has gone hard.

A slightly better oven-baked pancake

Oven-baked pancakes—the ingredients can be found in the cupboard, they can be easily whisked together, and voilà, happy children. It's a classic win-win dish. (For those who add a handful of beans we call it a win-win-win dish.)

Serves 4

1 (14.5 ounce) can cooked white beans
    (380 grams, drained weight 230 grams)
2½ cups whole milk
4 eggs
1¼ cups sifted spelt flour
1 teaspoon salt
Butter for greasing

Instructions:
1. Heat the oven to 450°F.
2. Discard the brine, rinse, and leave the beans to drain. Mix the beans into a paste with half the milk.
3. Mix the rest of the milk, eggs, flour, and salt into the bean/milk mix. Whisk into a smooth batter.
4. Pour the batter into a greased roasting pan, around 12 x 16 inches in size.
5. Bake the pancake in the middle of the oven for 25 to 30 minutes or until it has turned a nice color. Leave it for a few minutes to settle before cutting.

ADD FLAVOR TO THE PANCAKE!

Your kids probably won't jump for joy if you start to sprinkle the pancake with black cabbage and the like, but why not push the boundaries anyway? Remove the stalk from 1¾ ounces of black cabbage and place the leaves in a bowl. Sprinkle a pinch of flaked salt on top and add ½ tablespoon olive oil. Squeeze the cabbage with clean hands to soften it. Cut two red apples into thin wedges. Place the cabbage and apple evenly over the pancake before baking it in the oven. Bake according to the instructions above.

CAKES, PIES & BARS

Make a spicy banana cake with kidney beans, mix some white beans into a moist almond cake, or give blueberry bars an extra boost with lentils. And I promise you, no one will ever know that the chocolate cookies mostly contain black beans and hazelnuts.

Blueberry bars with
cinnamon & cardamom (GLUTEN-FREE)

Suddenly snack bars are everywhere, but they certainly aren't cheap. So why not make your own with lentils? This was my first attempt and they are ten times better than store-bought bars (she says humbly).

12 bars

½ cup dried, black lentils (70 grams)

10 dates (around 125 grams)

½ cup dried blueberries (or cranberries)

⅔ cup pumpkin seeds

½ cup desiccated coconut

1 tablespoon honey

3 tablespoons chia seeds

2 egg whites

½ teaspoon ground cinnamon

½ teaspoon ground cardamom

1 teaspoon flaked salt

Instructions:

1. Rinse the black lentils and leave to soak overnight or for at least 12 hours.
2. Heat the oven to 300°F.
3. Discard the water, rinse, and leave the lentils to drain.
4. Roast the lentils in a dry frying pan while stirring on medium heat for around 10 minutes or until they are dry and crunchy.
5. Remove the pits from the dates.
6. Place the dried blueberries, pumpkin seeds, dates, desiccated coconut, honey, chia seeds, egg whites, cinnamon, and cardamom in a food processor and blend to a smooth batter.
7. Add in the lentils and flaked salt and mix quickly to blend.
8. Press the batter into a loaf pan covered in parchment paper, around 10 x 4 inches.
9. Bake in the middle of the oven for 40 minutes. Leave to cool.
10. Cut into 12 pieces.
11. The bars are best when stored in the freezer.

Mango bars
with red lentils (GLUTEN-FREE)

When you've eaten a sweet date snack too many and start to angle for the dried mango, you need a balance of sweet and sour in your life—and a pinch of flaked salt.

20 bars

¼ cup dried red lentils (40 grams)
7 ounces dried mango (200 grams)
8 fresh dates (around 3½ ounces)
¼ cup chia seeds
½ cup salted peanuts
Around 2 tablespoons coconut oil
½ teaspoon flaked salt

Instructions:

1. Rinse the lentils and leave to soak overnight or for at least 12 hours.
2. Discard the water, rinse, and leave the lentils to drain.
3. Roast the lentils in a dry frying pan while stirring on medium heat for around 10 minutes or until the lentils are dry and crunchy.
4. Cut the mango into small pieces and remove the pits from the dates.
5. Place the mango, dates, chia seeds, peanuts, and coconut oil in a food processor and blend to make fine breadcrumbs.
6. Add the lentils and flaked salt and briefly mix. Press the mixture into a loaf pan covered in parchment paper, around 10 x 4 inches. Leave in the fridge for at least 4 hours.
7. Cut into 20 pieces.
8. The bars are best stored in the freezer.

Chocolate balls
with banana chips (GLUTEN-FREE)

Chocolate and banana work great together and lentils and rolled oats are filling. This is the point where I tell you that these balls are perfect before a workout (but, honestly, I'd rather have one with a cup of coffee on the sofa).

15 balls

½ cup dried black lentils (80 grams)

12 fresh dates (around 5.3 ounces)

¾ cup almonds

1 tablespoon coconut oil

2 tablespoons cocoa powder

¼–⅓ cup water

¾ cup rolled oats

½ teaspoon flaked salt

½ cup banana chips

Banana chips or desiccated coconut for rolling

Instructions:

1. Rinse the black lentils and leave to soak overnight or for at least 12 hours.
2. Discard the water, rinse, and leave the lentils to drain.
3. Roast the lentils on medium heat in a dry frying pan while stirring for around 10 minutes or until they are dry and crunchy.
4. Remove the pits from the dates.
5. Mix the almonds, dates, coconut oil, cocoa powder, and water in a food processor to make a smooth paste. Add in rolled oats, lentils, and flaked salt and quickly blend.
6. Crush the banana chips with your hands to make rough crumbs and add to the mixture.
7. Roll the mixture into 15 balls. You can roll the balls in more crushed banana chips or desiccated coconut if you like. Place in the freezer for at least 4 hours.
8. The balls are best kept in the freezer.

Black bean brownies
with peanuts (GLUTEN-FREE)

If you love a chocolate truffle, you will love this dense brownie with a rich chocolate taste.

15 pieces

1 (14.5 ounce) can cooked black beans
    (380 grams, drained weight 230 grams)
1¾ ounces butter (50 grams)
3 eggs
⅓ cup cocoa powder
1 pinch salt
½ teaspoon vanilla extract
⅔ cup raw sugar
5.3 ounces dark chocolate (70% cacao)
    (150 grams)
½ cup salted peanuts
Melted dark chocolate for garnishing (optional)

Instructions:

1. Heat the oven to 350°F.
2. Discard the brine from the beans, rinse, and leave to drain.
3. Melt the butter and leave to cool slightly.
4. Mix the beans and eggs into a paste. Add butter, cocoa powder, salt, vanilla extract, and raw sugar. Mix into a smooth batter.
5. Break the chocolate into pieces and melt carefully in the microwave.
6. Pour the melted chocolate into the batter and quickly stir. Pour the batter into a greased roasting pan, around 10 x 8 inches. Place the peanuts evenly on top.
7. Bake in the middle of the oven for 30 minutes or until the brownies have set.
8. Drizzle with some melted dark chocolate if you like.

Black bean chocolate cookies (GLUTEN-FREE)

With beans and hazelnut butter, you don't need flour, butter, or eggs in this dough.

16 cookies

1¼ cups roasted hazelnuts (150 grams)
    or 5.3 ounces hazelnut butter
1 (14.5 ounce) can cooked black beans
    (380 grams, drained weight around
    230 grams)
⅓ cup raw sugar
¼ cup cocoa powder
1 teaspoon vanilla extract
1 teaspoon baking powder
½ teaspoon flaked salt
Chopped hazelnuts for sprinkling

Instructions:

1. Heat the oven to 350°F.
2. If making your own hazelnut butter, place the roasted hazelnuts in a food processor and mix until the nuts have turned into "nut butter." It can take a while depending on the power of your food processor. If the nuts stick along the edges, push them down with a spatula now and again and keep mixing.
3. Discard the brine, rinse, and drain the beans thoroughly.
4. Add beans, sugar, cocoa powder, vanilla extract, baking powder, and flaked salt into the food processor and mix into a smooth dough.
5. Shape the dough into two long pieces and place on a baking pan covered in parchment paper. Sprinkle some chopped nuts on top and carefully press into the dough using your hands.
6. Bake in the middle of the oven for 15 to 20 minutes.
7. Cut at an angle over the long pieces and leave to cool on a cooling rack.
8. The cookies are best stored in the freezer.

Tahini cookies
with ginger (GLUTEN-FREE)

My plan was to make a classic cookie but it turned into more of a Middle Eastern cookie. It's great to serve with a hot drink anyway and pairs with coffee as well as a sweet mint tea.

20 cookies

1 (14.5 ounce) can cooked white beans (380 grams, drained weight around 230 grams)
1⅔ cups almond flour (200 grams)
¼ cup tahini paste
½ cup raw sugar
1 teaspoon vanilla extract
1½ teaspoons ground ginger
1 teaspoon baking powder
1 teaspoon flaked salt
Chopped pistachio nuts for sprinkling

Instructions:

1. Heat the oven to 400°F.
2. Discard the brine, rinse, and leave the white beans to drain.
3. Place the beans, almond flour, tahini paste, raw sugar, vanilla extract, ground ginger, baking powder, and flaked salt in a food processor and mix into a smooth dough.
4. Divide into 20 pieces and roll into balls. Place onto a baking pan covered in parchment paper. Sprinkle pistachio nuts on top and lightly press into the dough with your hand so they stick.
5. Bake in the middle of the oven for 15 to 20 minutes. Leave to cool on a cooling rack.
6. Store the cookies in the freezer.

Peanut butter cookies (GLUTEN-FREE)

These are the first bean cookies I made and I was so surprised when the kids took a cookie each and immediately wanted another one. A hallelujah moment for this bean disciple!

16 cookies

1 (14.5 ounce) can cooked chickpeas
    (380 grams, drained weight around
    230 grams)
5.3 ounces salted peanuts (or 5.3 ounces
    peanut butter)
1 teaspoon vanilla extract
⅓ cup honey
1 teaspoon baking powder
1 pinch flaked salt
2.6 ounces chopped dark chocolate (75 grams)

Instructions:

1. Heat the oven to 350°F.
2. Discard the brine, rinse, and leave the chickpeas to drain thoroughly.
3. If making your own peanut butter, place the peanuts in a food processor and mix until the peanuts resemble "peanut butter." Add the chickpeas, vanilla extract, honey, baking powder, and flaked salt and mix into a smooth dough. Add the chocolate and quickly blend together.
4. Shape the dough into 16 balls. Place on a baking tray covered in parchment paper and slightly flatten the balls.
5. Bake in the middle of the oven for 20 minutes.
6. Leave to cool on a cooling rack. The cookies are best stored in the freezer.

Almond cake with berries (GLUTEN-FREE)

Like a moist Mazarin (Swedish almond tart). My advice is to not tell anyone that there are beans and potatoes in the cake before people taste it. No one will guess.

Serves 12

1 (14.5 ounce) can cooked white beans or chickpeas (380 grams, drained weight around 230 grams)
1¾ ounces butter (50 grams)
3 boiled potatoes, cold (200 grams)
⅔ cup almond flour (65 grams)
1 teaspoon baking powder
½ teaspoon vanilla extract
2 grated bitter almonds
3 eggs
¾ cup raw sugar
⅔ cup frozen or fresh berries, e.g. red currants, blueberries, or raspberries
1 teaspoon cornstarch
2 tablespoons slivered or chopped almonds
1 teaspoon powdered sugar (optional)

Instructions:

1. Heat the oven to 400°F.
2. Discard the brine, rinse, and leave the beans to drain.
3. Melt the butter and leave to cool slightly. Finely grate the boiled potatoes.
4. Mix the white beans into a smooth paste together with the butter.
5. Mix the almond flour with the baking powder, vanilla extract, and grated bitter almonds.
6. Whisk eggs and sugar until fluffy.
7. Pour the flour mix, bean butter, and potatoes into the whisked eggs. Mix into an even batter.
8. Pour the batter into a springform pan covered in parchment paper, around 10 inches in diameter. Mix the berries and cornstarch. Spread the berries and slivered or chopped almonds evenly over the cake.
9. Bake in the middle of the oven for around 30 to 35 minutes, or until the cake has set in the middle. Leave to cool.
10. Lightly dust the cake with powdered sugar and served with whipped cream.

Saffron cake
with figs (GLUTEN-FREE)

When fresh figs appear in the grocery store it's time to make a moist almond cake with saffron. If you get a craving outside of fig season, you can use plums, nectarines, or pears.

Serves 12

1 (14.5 ounce) can cooked white beans or chickpeas (380 grams, drained weight around 230 grams)

1¾ ounces of butter (50 grams)

½ lb. cold cooked potato (200 grams)

⅔ cup almond flour (65 grams)

1 teaspoon baking powder

½ teaspoon vanilla extract

2 grated bitter almonds

3 eggs

¾ cup raw sugar

¼ teaspoon saffron

3 fresh figs

Instructions:
1. Heat the oven to 400°F.
2. Discard the brine, rinse, and leave the beans to drain.
3. Melt the butter and leave to cool slightly. Finely grate the potato.
4. Mix the beans into a paste with the butter.
5. Mix the almond flour with baking powder, vanilla extract, and grated bitter almonds.
6. Whisk eggs, sugar, and saffron until fluffy.
7. Pour the flour mix, bean butter, and potato into the whisked eggs. Mix to make a smooth batter.
8. Pour the batter into a springform pan with a removable base, around 10 inches in diameter.
9. Cut the figs into 4 wedges and lightly press into the batter.
10. Bake in the middle of the oven for 30 to 35 minutes, or until the cake has set in the middle. Leave to cool.
11. Serve with whipped cream or crème fraiche if you like.

The cake pictured here was made using half a batch and was baked in a smaller pan, around 5 inches in diameter.

Coconut muffins
with lime (GLUTEN-FREE)

Coconut and lime are flavors that work well together. The muffins pictured here were made in an old muffin pan that was so pretty I couldn't resist using it, but it is easier to put the batter into small paper muffin liners.

15 muffins

1 (14.5 ounce) can cooked white beans or chickpeas (around 380 grams, drained weight around 230 grams)

2.6 ounces butter at room temperature (75 grams)

⅔ cup raw sugar

3 eggs

1⅔ cups desiccated coconut (140 grams)

1 teaspoon baking powder

½ teaspoon vanilla extract

1 teaspoon psyllium husk

2 teaspoons finely grated lime zest

1 tablespoon freshly squeezed lime juice

Desiccated coconut for sprinkling

Instructions:

1. Heat the oven to 400°F.
2. Discard the brine, rinse, and leave the beans to drain thoroughly. Mix them into a smooth paste by hand or with a hand blender.
3. Whisk the butter and sugar until fluffy. Add the eggs, one at a time, while still whisking.
4. Mix the coconut with the baking powder, vanilla extract, psyllium husk, and lime zest.
5. Add the bean paste, coconut mixture, and lime juice into the egg mixture. Whisk until smooth.
6. Dollop out the batter into 15 small muffin cases (the muffins pictured here were made without muffin cases and with half the amount of batter). Sprinkle some coconut on top.
7. Bake the muffins in the middle of the oven for around 15 minutes.
8. The muffins are best when stored in the freezer.

Apple pie with
coconut crumble (GLUTEN-FREE)

It makes me so happy to use lentils in the most unexpected dishes. Like making this crumble, for example. Try it, it really is delicious!

Serves 6

¼ cup dried red lentils (140 grams)
5 large apples
½ cup rolled oats (35 grams)
½ cup desiccated coconut (35 grams)
⅓ cup raw sugar
2 pinches flaked salt
1 teaspoon ground cinnamon
2.6 ounces butter (75 grams)
Butter for greasing

Instructions:

1. Rinse the red lentils and leave to soak overnight or for at least 12 hours.
2. Heat the oven to 400°F.
3. Core and cut the apples into smaller pieces. Place in a greased ovenproof dish, around 10 inches in diameter.
4. Place the drained lentils in a food processor together with the rolled oats, coconut, sugar, salt, and cinnamon. Blend until mixture resembles breadcrumbs. Cut the butter into pieces and add to the mixture. Quickly mix into a crumbly dough. Spread the crumble evenly over the apples.
5. Bake in the middle of the oven for around 35 minutes or until the apples are soft and the pie has a nice color. Serve with a dollop of cream or ice cream.

Banana bread (GLUTEN-FREE)

I challenged myself to make a banana bread recipe using beans. After several strange experiments, I can now proudly present to you a recipe that actually works.

1 loaf

1 (14.5 ounce) can kidney beans (380 grams, drained weight around 230 grams)
2 bananas (around 275 grams)
4.4 ounces butter at room temperature (125 grams)
½ cup brown sugar (90 grams)
2 eggs at room temperature
¾ cup oat flour (100 grams)
2 teaspoons baking powder
½ teaspoon salt
1 teaspoon ground cinnamon
1 teaspoon ground ginger
¾ cup walnuts
1 banana + 1 tablespoon brown sugar for garnishing

Instructions:

1. Heat the oven to 400°F.
2. Discard the brine, rinse, and leave the kidney beans to drain.
3. Mash the beans and bananas together.
4. Whisk the butter and brown sugar until fluffy. Add the eggs one at a time.
5. Mix the oat flour, baking powder, salt, cinnamon, and ginger.
6. Add the flour mixture and banana and bean mash to the butter cream. Fold with a spatula to blend.
7. Finally fold in the walnuts.
8. Pour the batter into a greased and floured loaf pan, around 8½ x 4½ x 2½ inches.
9. Halve the banana and place on top of the bread. Sprinkle the brown sugar on top.
10. Bake in the oven for around 40 minutes in the middle of the oven.
11. Leave to cool for 10 minutes before turning out the cake. Leave to completely cool on a cooling rack.

Chocolate & orange cake
with buckwheat crisp (GLUTEN-FREE)

It's amazing that you can make meringue from chickpea brine. Here I mix it all together so that both the chickpea meringue and the mixed chickpeas turn into a dense chocolate mousse on a crispy base made from roasted buckwheat, almond, and maple syrup.

Serves 12

Base:
¾ cup whole buckwheat
⅔ cup almonds
1 tablespoon canola oil
½ cup maple syrup
½ teaspoon flaked salt

Filling:
3½ ounces dark chocolate (70% cacao)
    (100 grams)
1 (14.5 ounce) can cooked chickpeas
    (380 grams, drained weight around
    230 grams)
½ cup raw sugar
1 tablespoon grated orange peel
Cocoa powder to sprinkle over the cake
    (optional)

You can keep some of the buckwheat crumble and sprinkle over the cake before serving. You can also garnish with some orange zest.

Instructions:

1. **Base:** Rinse the buckwheat in hot water for around 30 seconds. Cover with water and leave to soak overnight.
2. Discard the water from the buckwheat and rinse thoroughly until all the foam has disappeared.
3. Roast the almonds in a dry, hot frying pan.
4. Fry the buckwheat in oil in a frying pan on medium heat while stirring until it is dry and crispy. Leave to cool.
5. Place the buckwheat, almonds, canola oil, maple syrup, and flaked salt in a food processor and blend until the mixture resembles breadcrumbs.
6. Press the crumb mixture into a springform pan with a removable ring, around 8 inches (you can use a 10-inch one too but it will make a very thin cake). Place the base in the fridge for around 1 hour.

1. **Filling:** Melt the chocolate carefully in the microwave.
2. Remove the brine from the chickpeas and keep in a bowl.
3. Beat the brine, adding a little sugar at a time, until it becomes a firm meringue.
4. Mix the chickpeas into a smooth paste by hand or with a hand blender.
5. Fold the mixed chickpeas and the grated orange peel into the meringue and quickly whisk together.
6. Add the melted chocolate while still whisking and whisk into a smooth mousse.
7. Spread the mousse over the cake base. Place the cake in the freezer for at least 4 hours. Remove the cake at least half an hour before serving.
8. Dust some cocoa powder on top if you like.

Hazelnut galette
with plums

A crispy fruit galette with a hint of hazelnuts and cardamom. Fill it with plums or another fruit like nectarines, pears, or apple.

Serves 8

1 (14.5 ounce) can cooked white beans
    (380 grams, drained weight 230 grams)
1¾ ounces butter (50 grams)
1 egg
¾ cup sifted spelt flour
⅔ cup hazelnut flour
¼ cup raw sugar
½ teaspoon ground cardamom
1 pinch salt
10 plums
2 tablespoons raw sugar
Powdered sugar for dusting (optional)

Instructions:

1. Discard the brine, rinse, and leave the beans to drain. Mix them into a smooth paste by hand or with a hand blender.
2. Mix together the butter, egg, sifted spelt flour, hazelnut flour, raw sugar, and cardamom. Add the bean paste and quickly work into a smooth dough. Cover and let the dough rest in the fridge for around 20 minutes.
3. Heat the oven to 400°F.
4. Roll out the dough to a rectangle (or circle if you want to make a round galette) on a floured piece of parchment paper, around 12 inches in diameter. Place the paper in a baking pan.
5. Remove the pits from the plums, and cut the pitted plums into slices. Spread the fruit in a nice pattern over the base, around an inch from the edge. Fold in the edges and sprinkle some raw sugar on top.
6. Bake in the middle of the oven for around 30 minutes or until the galette is golden in color. Dust with powdered sugar if you like.

Index of recipes

Which beans do you have at home?

Conversion Charts

METRIC AND IMPERIAL CONVERSIONS
(These conversions are rounded for convenience)

Ingredient	Cups/Tablespoons/ Teaspoons	Ounces	Grams/Milliliters
Butter	1 cup/ 16 tablespoons/ 2 sticks	8 ounces	230 grams
Cheese, shredded	1 cup	4 ounces	110 grams
Cream cheese	1 tablespoon	0.5 ounce	14.5 grams
Cornstarch	1 tablespoon	0.3 ounce	8 grams
Flour, all-purpose	1 cup/1 tablespoon	4.5 ounces/0.3 ounce	125 grams/8 grams
Flour, whole wheat	1 cup	4 ounces	120 grams
Fruit, dried	1 cup	4 ounces	120 grams
Fruits or veggies, chopped	1 cup	5 to 7 ounces	145 to 200 grams
Fruits or veggies, pureed	1 cup	8.5 ounces	245 grams
Honey, maple syrup, or corn syrup	1 tablespoon	0.75 ounce	20 grams
Liquids: cream, milk, water, or juice	1 cup	8 fluid ounces	240 milliliters
Oats	1 cup	5.5 ounces	150 grams
Salt	1 teaspoon	0.2 ounce	6 grams
Spices: cinnamon, cloves, ginger, or nutmeg (ground)	1 teaspoon	0.2 ounce	5 milliliters
Sugar, brown, firmly packed	1 cup	7 ounces	200 grams
Sugar, white	1 cup/1 tablespoon	7 ounces/0.5 ounce	200 grams/12.5 grams
Vanilla extract	1 teaspoon	0.2 ounce	4 grams

OVEN TEMPERATURES

Fahrenheit	Celsius	Gas Mark
225°	110°	¼
250°	120°	½
275°	140°	1
300°	150°	2
325°	160°	3
350°	180°	4
375°	190°	5
400°	200°	6
425°	220°	7
450°	230°	8

Skyhorse Publishing books may be purchased in bulk at special discounts for sales promotion, corporate gifts, fund-raising, or educational purposes. Special editions can also be created to specifications. For details, contact the Special Sales Department, Skyhorse Publishing, 307 West 36th Street, 11th Floor, New York, NY 10018 or info@skyhorsepublishing.com.

Skyhorse® and Skyhorse Publishing® are registered trademarks of Skyhorse Publishing, Inc.®, a Delaware corporation.

Visit our website at www.skyhorsepublishing.com.

10 9 8 7 6 5 4 3 2 1

Library of Congress Cataloging-in-Publication Data is available on file.

Cover design by Daniel Brount
Cover photo by Lennart Weibull

Print ISBN: 978-1-5107-4628-2
Ebook ISBN: 978-1-5107-4630-5

Printed in China